Foreword by His Holiness The Dalai Lama

Leaf Talks Peace
Buddha's Message of Harmony

Written by
Priya Kumari

Illustrated by
Anusha Santosh

Eternal Tree Books

Publisher's Cataloging-in-Publication data

Names: Kumari, Priya, 1985-, author. | Santosh, Anusha, illustrator. | Bstan-'dzin-rgya-mtsho, Dalai Lama XIV, 1935-, foreword author.
Title: Leaf talks peace : Buddha's message of harmony / written by Priya Kumari ; illustrated by Anusha Santosh ; foreword by Prof. Lokesh Chandra.
Description: East Brunswick, NJ: Eternal Tree Books, 2022. | Summary: Buddha's message of interdependent origination of life – as he saw in a leaf – for achieving social, ecological and individual peace, written from the perspective of a leaf.
Identifiers: LCCN: 2021931093 | ISBN: 978-1-953384-13-3 (ebook) | ISBN: 978-1-953384-23-2 (pbk.) | 978-1-953384-24-9 (Hardcover)
Subjects: LCSH Buddhism--Juvenile literature. | Gautama Buddha--Juvenile literature. | Bodhi tree--Juvenile literature. | Conduct of life--Juvenile literature. | CYAC Buddhism. | Gautama Buddha. | Bodhi tree. | Conduct of life. | JUVENILE NONFICTION / Religion / Buddhism | JUVENILE NONFICTION / Social Topics / Values & Virtues
Classification: LCC BQ4022 .K86 2022 | DDC 294.3--dc23

ISBN: 978-1-953384-13-3 (ebook)
ISBN: 978-1-953384-23-2 (paperback)
ISBN: 978-1-953384-24-9 (hardcover)
Library of Congress Control Number: 2021931093

First edition 2022

Edited by David Aretha

Printed in India
Published by Eternal Tree Books LLC
East Brunswick, NJ, USA
www.eternaltreebooks.com

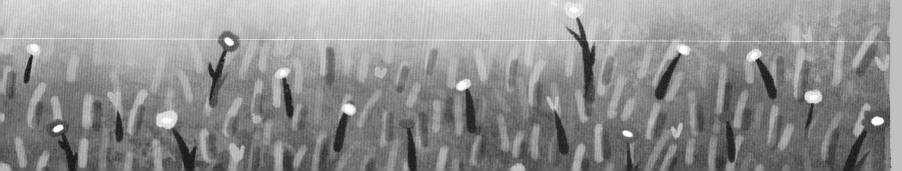

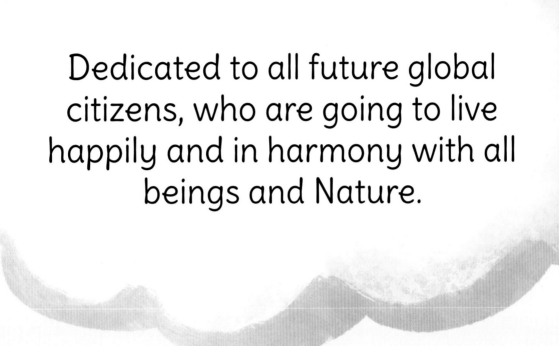

Dedicated to all future global citizens, who are going to live happily and in harmony with all beings and Nature.

THE DALAI LAMA

FOREWORD

Buddha Shakyamuni was born under a tree, he attained enlightenment under a tree, and he also passed away under a tree. He forbade his monastic followers to cut living plants, cause damage to seeds, or to defile fresh green grass.

The preservation of our planet, our only home, is crucial to our survival. Its exploitation is leading to extreme climatic conditions that are exhausting the natural resources we depend on to survive. It is therefore vital that we understand the interdependent relationship we share with nature. This should be introduced to our younger generation from an early age.

Priya Kumari's "Leaf Talks Peace" is a beautifully illustrated book that teaches children the importance of living in harmony with nature and with all forms of life. I hope that it will contribute to a better awareness of the responsibility each of us has to protect our environment in order to insure the survival of humanity.

23 March 2021

THE TWELFTH TAI SITUPA

Message

"A beautiful children's book conveying Buddha's message of interdependent origination of life. The author has elegantly depicted life with the help of a leaf. Rhyming words and deeply thought illustrations make this book unique. It is a jewel of thoughts as it encourages young readers to protect cultural diversity and perceive themselves a reflection of harmony seen in nature."

H.H. The Kenting Tai Situpa
The Supreme Head of the Palpung Institution of Buddha Dharma
Palpung Sherabling Monastic Seat
Himachal Pradesh, INDIA

PALPUNG SHERABLING MONASTIC SEAT
P.O. Upper Bhattu Via Baijnath-176125, District Kangra, Himachal Pradesh, India
www.palpung.org

Hi! My name is Harmony.
I am a leaf, green 'n' tiny.

I live on this tree, Bodhi.
I will now tell you a story.

Once, Buddha sat under Bodhi.
I began dancing in the sky.
I wished he could talk to me.
He looked at me so deeply.

He saw the Sun in me.

He saw the stars in me.

Light of them is life in me.
Warmth of them lives in me.

He saw the clouds in me.
He saw the rain in me.

Waters of them is life in me.

Void of them is end of me.

He saw the soil in me.
He saw the Earth in me.

He saw the time in me.
He saw the space in me.

He saw a mind in me.
He saw a miracle in me.

He saw a web of wonders in me.
saw the whole universe in me.

No fear in me,
No tears in me.
No "I" in me,
No "who" in me.
All are one in me.

I talk peace in me.
Sing harmony in me.
The dance of me,
Is the message of me.

See the plurality in me,
Human solidarity in me.

Protect the "many" in me.
Protect the "we" in me.

Protect the oneness in me.
Protect the harmony in me.
Spread the happiness of me.
Spread the harmony of me.

Remember the name is Harmony.
I am any leaf, big 'n' tiny.

Message

This enchanting presentation of our Being emerging from the water and wind, floating across the earth and the sky, is the heart of our perception of Life. This book by Priya Kumari puts subtle echoes of our culture in the simple elegance of illustrations to fascinate tender minds. The 'me' is the flowering heart of nature. When snow thaws in the Himalayas, pebbles rolling down the torrents of River Gandaki became our sacred Shaligrams. They are divine consciousness that pervades life with its invisible presence.

The moment we ponder on a phenomenon it becomes a value, a dharma to enrich lives with its inherent beauty. In his meditation, Siddhartha saw hidden symbols in tiny leaves. He saw the shade of panhuman values in those symbols. He saw the whole of life and nature linked up in a seamless web. In the same way, human solidarity will emerge from a shared world, a world where diversity is respected, where interdependence is the root of consciousness, where the Absolute is subjected to an ever-dynamic ascension to higher and higher absolutes in the plural and in transition in all ages.

Our great epic Ramayana welled forth when great poet Valmiki was aggrieved at the agony of one of a lovelorn couple of Krauncha birds falling down, shot by a hunter. It became the shloka or glory of language to pen the Ramayana. Dear children, this lovely book is your shloka, your hymn to tread the glory of life. Your minds will mingle with the Divine in the many miles you shall go. These simple pictures are the poetry of peace in the sinews of nature.

Lokesh Chandra

Prof. Lokesh Chandra
Director, International Academy of Indian Culture
Formerly President ICCR and Member of Parliament, India

Author's Note

Harmony can happen in the world when there is peace between humans, peace with nature, and peace within ourselves. It can happen when differences are respected, when everyone acknowledges interdependent origination of life, and when there are no absolute dogmas but constant evolution of thoughts. A world where life is supreme, where there is a meaningful arrangement of different orders. Humans can live together only in a pluralism where diversity and change are owned and respected.

This illustrated poem gives a clear message of harmony and peace mentioned in Buddhist Agamas, ancient texts. Inspired by Prof. Lokesh Chandra, I wrote this poem to tell young children about the importance of living harmoniously.

The poem takes us back in time to the Bodhi tree where Buddha is meditating. He observes how a Peepal leaf gives a message of interdependent origination of life. He sees the Sun, the Earth, clouds, time, space, and consciousness in a leaf. There is a peaceful co-existence of all. A leaf cannot survive without any of these different elements. He finds the entire universe breathing happily in a leaf. The leaf, a symbol of human well-being, comes from interdependence and not from coercion.

This is nothing but a miracle as all lives and nature are arranged peacefully. Human solidarity and harmony can happen when there is ecological peace, social peace, and individual peace, in a world where there is selflessness and acceptance of the many. We must protect this life-giving light of interdependence and plurality.

Ashtamangala
Eight auspicious symbols

 The Conch awakens us from deep slumber and dispels ignorance.

 The Endless Knot gives the message of unity and interdependent origination.

 The Wheel of Dharma inculcates morality and spreads the message of well-being.

 The Victory Banner symbolizes victory of knowledge over ignorance.

 The Parasol protects all beings from illness and harm.

 The Pair of Golden Fish instills fearlessness and conveys freedom of movement.

 The Lotus brings purity in our thoughts and actions.

 The Treasure Vase indicates fulfillment of spiritual and material wishes.

Guidance for Teachers and Parents

The objective of this book is to inculcate a sense of harmony and care in young readers. There are three messages for readers.

1. Social peace: It is important to see how so many elements live in a leaf. They all live in harmony inside a leaf. In the same way we need to live in harmony with fellow beings despite their differences as this is a shared world.

2. Spiritual peace: Similar to how a leaf is peaceful and complete within we also need to be happy within.

3. Ecological peace: We need to live in harmony with nature and do everything to protect it.

Before reading the story, teachers or parents can start with a discussion of who Buddha was. They can refer to him as a prince who left his palace to meditate. He wanted to meditate to find solutions to suffering and sadness. Thus, began his journey from being Prince Siddhartha to becoming the Buddha. "Buddha" means the one who is enlightened, one whose questions have been answered. This is from the Sanskrit word "Bodhi," meaning enlightenment.

After the story is read, the following discussions can be carried out.

1. **What is a Bodhi Tree?**
It is a Peepal tree under which Buddha attained enlightenment. Peepal trees are incredibly significant in the Indian tradition. They have therapeutic properties and are a tremendous source of oxygen. Such trees also create an ambience conducive to meditation and learning. Therefore, sages chose such trees to meditate under. As the seeker attains enlightenment, the tree also attains divinity. This is reflected in the name Bodhi, meaning enlightenment.

2. **Why did Buddha see the Sun in a leaf?**
A leaf needs the Sun to grow. Without its light and warmth, there would be no leaf.

3. **Why did he find the presence of the Earth in a leaf?**

A leaf also needs nutrition from the soil to grow, so the Earth also plays an important role in bringing a leaf to life.

4. **Why did he see the presence of clouds in a leaf?**

Clouds bring rain and rain brings water for the leaves to grow. So, a leaf also depends on water to survive.

5. **How does a leaf have a mind or consciousness?**

A tiny seed pushes itself up from the soil in a form of a seedling to be able to get energy from the Sun. Therefore, trees and plants also have consciousness or mind. Sunflowers turn toward the Sun because there is a consciousness within the flowers. Similarly, creepers climb without anyone helping them do so.

6. **Why does Buddha find the presence of time and space in a leaf?**

A leaf grows over time. One plants a small sapling, and it grows step by step into a huge tree. This process of growing happens with time, so Buddha saw the dependence on time as well for the leaf to exist. Also, the size of a leaf grows bigger and it takes more space. So, he also saw the element of space living in a leaf.

7. **Why does the author say there is neither fear nor "I" in a leaf? What is the meaning of protecting "we" and "many" in a leaf?**

Since a leaf is a product of so many elements, there is interdependent origination of leaf/life. We can say spiritually that all elements exist in a leaf. Light, soil, water, mind, time, and space do not fight amongst themselves but live together in a leaf, there is no fear. They all depend on each other for a leaf to exist. So "I" is not there but "we" is there in a leaf. In the same way we all live together in a shared world. We must share the world with fellow humans irrespective of their culture, color, race, language, or ethnicity. With this sharing, happiness will exist. This "we" or togetherness or plurality must be protected for life to prosper.

8. **What is the message of the leaf, Harmony?**

The author is trying to tell readers that when they see any leaf, they should remind themselves of the importance of living in harmony with everyone, letting everyone express their ways of living, be accommodative, and keep life at the center of all action. A leaf should remind us to turn inward and find happiness within. A leaf should encourage us to protect nature.

Activities

Teachers can encourage a discussion on holidays. Kids can talk about their main holidays and explain what they like the most about them. This will help them understand and learn about each other's culture and way of thinking. They can discuss different languages. The more we discuss these things the more inclusive and respectful our society will be.

To discuss individual peace, one can encourage children to practice mindfulness and be peaceful within, just like a leaf that dances happily when the wind blows. Teachers can also talk about coloring activities to reduce stress, listening to soothing music, chanting mantras, and being with nature.

To explain ecological peace, children can be motivated to protect natural resources and prevent pollution in whichever way they can. The three Rs can be discussed. They can Reduce the use of single-use plastics in their daily lives to be respectful towards nature. They can be encouraged to switch off extra lights in their homes. Children can also be encouraged to Recycle and Reuse. These small things will make them more mindful of their dependence on nature.

This book is an attempt to help global citizens become more conscious. It is important to tell our children these important things at an early age, so they become more mindful adults.